THE MESSERSCHMITT BF 109 VOL. 2

Bf 109C-1 of a fighter training school in the winter of 1940-1941.

Fritz X. Kobel and Jakob Maria Mathmann

Schiffer Military History
Atglen, PA

PHOTO CREDITS

Archive of the Aviation History Research Group
Dressel Photo and Information Service
Daimler-Benz Aerospace, Munich

FAG Frankfurt	NASM, Washington D.C.
W. Green	H. Nowarra (+)
P. Heck	W. Radinger (via Dressel)
H.F. Hofmann	S. Schröder
W. Holzmann	A. Stolzenberg
G. Lang	USAF, Dayton, Ohio
B. Lange	H. Voigt
M. Lorant	C.L. Wahl
Griehl Aviation Archive	B. Werner
R.P. Lutz Jr. (via Griehl)	W. Winweile
H. Müller	

A Bf 109G captured by the Soviets; the aircraft had previously been flown by the pilots of 15 (Kroat.)/JG 52, a unit consisting of Croatian personnel.

BIBLIOGRAPHY

J.R. Beaman: Messerschmitt Bf 109 in Action, Squadron Photo Album # 44, Texas 1980.

J.R. Beaman: Messerschmitt Bf 109 in Action, Squadron Photo Album # 57, Texas 1983.

M. Griehl: Messerschmitt G/K, Profile No. 5, Illertissen.

OKL, GdJ-Grp.Qu., Br.B.Nr. 1561/45 g.Kdos. (op) of 20/03/1945.

OKL, Lw.-Führungsstab, Nr. 937/45 g.Kdos. (op) of 08/02/1945.

Komm.Gen.d.Dt.Lw. in Italien, Qu/Ib, Nr. 501/45, g.Kdos. of 27/03/1945.

Jagdgeschwader 6, Ia - Br.B.Nr. 10524/45 geh. of 23/03/1945.

Archive of the Aviation History Research Group

H.J. Ebert: Die deutsche Luftfahrtgeschichte, Vol. 17, Bonn 1992.

R. Kosin: Die deutsche Luftfahrt, Vol. 4, Koblenz 1990.

Translated from the German by David Johnston.

Copyright © 1996 by Schiffer Publishing Ltd.

Printed in China.
ISBN: 0-88740-919-9

This book was originally published under the title,
Waffen Arsenal- Messerschmitt Bf 109 Im Einsatz
by Podzun-Pallas Verlag.

We are interested in hearing from authors with book ideas on related topics.

Published by Schiffer Publishing Ltd.
77 Lower Valley Road
Atglen, PA 19310
Please write for a free catalog.
This book may be purchased from the publisher.
Please include $2.95 postage.
Try your bookstore first.

MESSERSCHMITT BF 109

The entry of the Bayerische Flugzeugwerke (BFW) into the field of military aircraft construction was not without complications. Theo Croneiss, since October 1933 chairman of the supervisory board of BFW and thus quasi-responsible for the creation of an aviation industry in Bavaria, received a confidential letter from Hermann Göring, in which the latter wrote that there was a requirement for the development of an airliner and a single-seat, high-speed courier aircraft. He went on to say that a large aircraft factory in Augsburg was very desirable. Although initially only the firms of Arado, Focke-Wulf and Heinkel received development contracts for a light fighter - the "Armaments Aircraft III" - Willy Messerschmitt received a very clear indication from the RLM that he too was to participate in fighter aircraft development.

After reviewing the specification Messerschmitt drove to Berlin and declared: "With a fighter such as this you'll never be able to shoot down a high-speed bomber, such as is already technically possible and which will certainly come someday." Chief of Staff Wever subsequently instructed Messerschmitt to develop a fighter based on his own concepts.

Beginning in early March 1934, one of the heads of the project bureau, Robert Lusser, consulted with the RLM to clarify detail questions concerning the choice of power plants (Jumo 210A or BMW 116) and other equipment. Some importance was placed on providing the aircraft with folding wings. To accommodate this feature, the aircraft's undercarriage legs were attached to the fuselage. This resulted in a narrow track which later led to numerous takeoff and landing accidents. Concerning the aircraft's armament, there were several alternatives to choose from:

- one MG C 30 (20 mm) firing through the hollow shaft of the engine
- two MG 17 (7.9 mm firing through the propeller disc
- two MG 17 (7.9 mm) and one engine-mounted MG-FF (20 mm)

Under the direction of Richard Bauer, design work on the Bf 109 began in August 1934. Construction of the first prototype started in December of the same year. Flugapitän Hans Dietrich Knoetzsch, then BFW's chief test pilot, began taxing trials with the Bf 109A (D-IABI) in May 1935. As the Bf 109 V1, this machine should have gone to the Erprobungsstelle (E-Stelle, or testing station) at Rechlin for technical testing; but Knoetzsch crashed the aircraft resulting in the loss of the prototype for some time. The Bf 109 V2 first flew in October 1935 followed by the third prototype in June 1936. The type gained its first operational experience in the Spanish Civil War beginning in late 1936, when the Bf 109 V3 through V5 were sent to Spain.

The Jumo 210 A in-line engine was the standard power plant up to the Bf 109 V4 (B-01); a Jumo 210 B was installed in the Bf 109 V5 (B-02). Following a pre-production series of ten aircraft with the Jumo 210 C power plant, in February 1937 the first Bf 109B-1 with the Jumo 210 Da was delivered at Augsburg-Haunstetten; these aircraft were assigned to II/JG 132 Richthofen which was based at Jüterbog-Damm near Berlin. In April 1937 these machines were transferred to the Condor Legion's 2/J88 in Spain to replace that unit's He 51 biplanes. Forty Bf 109B-1 and B-2 fighters were ultimately used in action there.

At the time of the German entry into Austria on March 12, 1938, the Luftwaffe had only six Jagdgruppen equipped with the Bf 109B. These were I/JG 131 at Jesau, I/JG 132 at Döberitz, II/JG 132 at Jüterbog-Damm, I/JG 234 at Cologne, II/JG 234 at Düsseldorf, and I/JG 136 at Wiesbaden-Erbenheim. I/JG 136 based at Eger-Marienbad was equipped with the He 51 C-2. Equipped with the Ar 68 were I/JG 134 at Dortmund, II/JG 134 at Werl, I/JG 135 at Aibling, I/JG 137 at Bernburg, and I/JG 133 at Mannheim.

The Bf 109 V7 on display at the air meet held in Dübendorf.

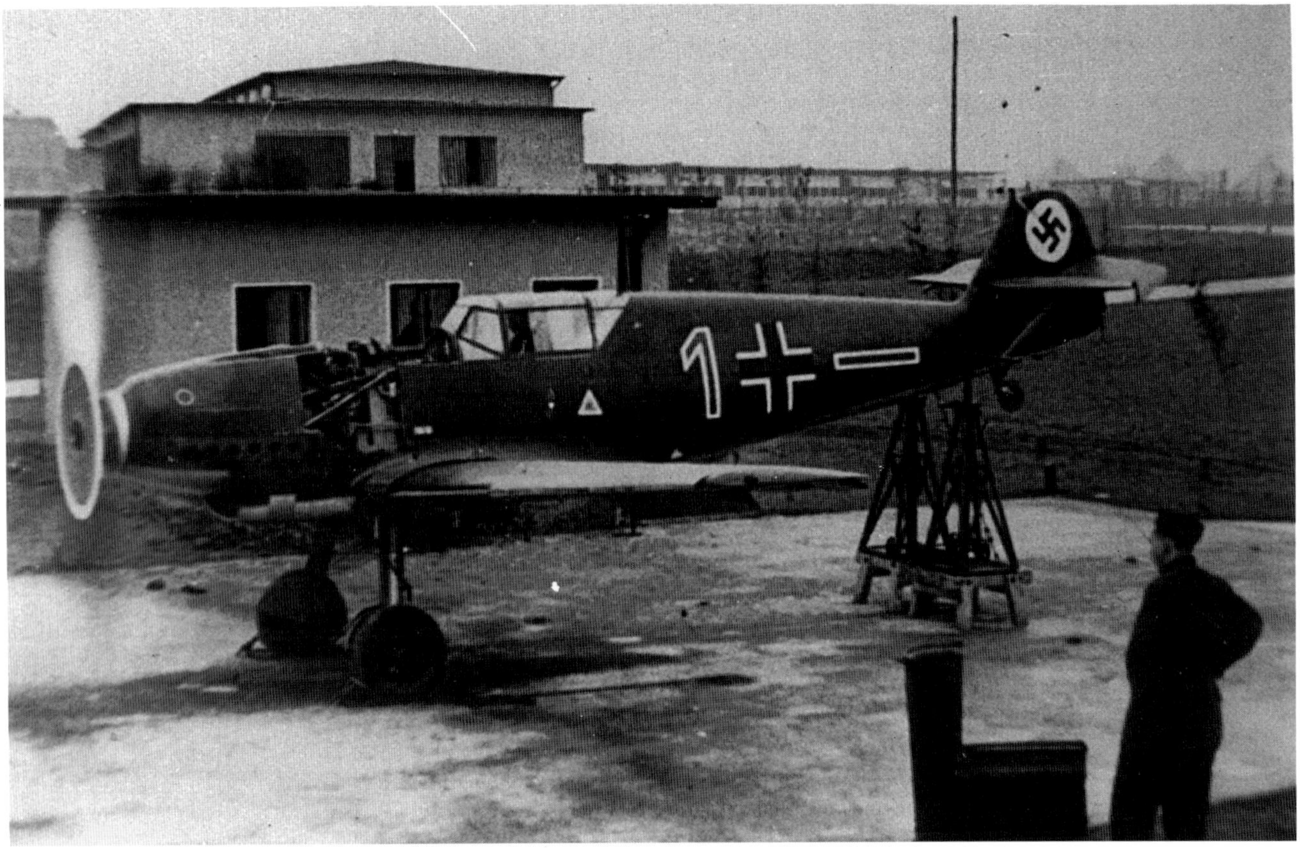

The Bf 109B-1 served with the fighter units JG 131, JG 132, JG 234 and JG 334.

Bottom:

This Bf 109B-2 was passed on to a training unit when its days as a front-line fighter were over.

Beginning in early 1938, the Jumo 210 Ga-powered Bf 109C began replacing the two B-series types then in service. In addition to the change of engine, the C-series also saw the beginning of experiments with a heavier armament (20-mm MG FF/M engine-mounted cannon and MG 17s in the wings). Some of these tests were carried out in Spain. Not until the summer of 1938 did a unit based in Germany, I/JG 132, reequip with the Bf 109C. By July 1938 it was joined by III/JG 132 at Jüterbog-Damm (formed with Austrian personnel), IV/JG 132 at Werneuchen, IV/JG 134 at Dortmund, II/JG 135 at Aibling, II/JG 137 at Zerbst, I/JG 138 (partial) at Aspern near Vienna, JG 234 at Düsseldorf, and III/JG 334 at Mannheim.

The more powerful DB 600 engine was supposed to be installed in the Bf 109D series as soon as it was ready for service use. However, as these engines were more urgently needed for bomber production (He 111), the Bf 109D-1 was produced as an interim solution powered by a Jumo 210 Da. At least one Bf 109D "Dora" was fitted with a DB 600 engine - solely for propaganda purposes, however.

With quantity production of the DB 601 about to begin, in the summer of 1938 the Bf 109 V14 and V15 were equipped to serve as test beds for use of this power plant in the future Bf 109E series. Eight Bf 109E machines with the new engine followed in the autumn of the same year.

A total of 36 Bf 109D-1 fighters were sent to Spain. The aircraft bore the codes 6.51 to 6.86.

Left: Powered by a Jumo 210, the Bf 109D-1 was used primarily by pilot training schools.

5

Apart from the DB 601 Aa, the Bf 109E exhibited a number of obvious differences from the preceding variants in the area of the engine cowling and oil-cooler installation. The standard armament of the Bf 109C/D (four MG 17 machine-guns) was retained by the Bf 109E-1 series. The Bf 109E-2 was supposed to see the return of the MG FF engine-mounted cannon. In spite of various improvements, weapons tests carried out by JG 27 were unsuccessful on account of vibration and recoil problems. The Bf 109E-2 did not enter series production.

Meanwhile another reorganization of the flying units took place. On 1 September 1939 the Bf 109 was in service with the following units:

LUFTFLOTTE 2 (Air Fleet 2) (NORTHWEST GERMANY)

UNIT	BASE	NUMBER
I/JG 26	Cologne-Ostheim	48
II/JG 26	Düsseldorf	48
10(N)/JG 26	Düsseldorf	9
I/ZG 26	Dortmund	52
II/ZG 26	Werl	48
III/ZG 26	Lippstadt	49
(JGr 126)		

LUFTFLOTTE 3 (Air Fleet 3) (SOUTHWEST GERMANY)

UNIT	BASE	NUMBER
I/JG 51	Bad Aibling	47
I/JG 52	Böblingen	39
I/JG 53	Wiesbaden-Erbenheim	51
II/JG 53	Mannheim-Sandhofen	43
1 and 2/JG 70	Nuremberg	24
1/JG 71	Friedrichshafen	15
2/JG 71	Friedrichshafen	24

LUFTWAFFEN LEHRDIVISION (Luftwaffe Training Division)

UNIT	BASE	NUMBER
Stab/LG 2	Jüterbog-Damm	3
I(J)/LG 2	Garz	36
II(N)/LG 2	Garz	10

LUFTFLOTTE 1 (Air Fleet 1) (NORTH GERMANY)

UNIT	BASE	NUMBER
I/JG 1	Seerappen	54
I/JG 21	Jesau	29
I/JG 2	Döberitz	42
10(N)/JG 20	Fürstenwalde	9
1 and 2/JG 20	Fürstenwalde	21
Stab/JG 3	Bernburg	3
I/JG 3	Zerbst	48
JGr 101 (ZG 1)	Fürstenwalde	36
JGr 102 (ZG 2)	Bernburg	44

LUFTFLOTTE 4 (Air Fleet 4) (SOUTHEAST GERMANY AUSTRIA, BOHEMIA AND MORAVIA)

UNIT	BASE	NUMBER
I/JG 76	Vienna-Aspern	49
I/JG 77	Breslau	50
II/JG 77	Pilsen	50
JGr 176 (ZG 76)	Gablingen	40

FLEET AIR ARM (BALTIC)

UNIT 4TB	BASE	NUMBER
5(J)/TrGr 186	Kiel-Holtenau	12
6(J)/TrGr 186	Kiel-Holtenau	12

Front view of a Bf 109D-1 of a pilot training school in central Germany.

Bf 109E-1 of III/JG 51 photographed during the winter of 1939/1940.

Filling the fuel tank of a Bf 109E-1 of 3/JG 51. The aircraft was equipped with a DB 601 Aa in-line engine.

A Bf 109E-1 of the 1st Staffel of Jagdgeschwader 51 following a crash near Braunschweig.

The obvious need to strengthen the armament of the Messerschmitt fighter resulted in the Bf 109E-3. Two MG FF 20-mm cannon replaced the pair of wing-mounted MG 17 machine-guns. Deliveries of the aircraft to the units began with II/JG 54 in the autumn of 1939. By April 1940, seventeen Gruppen in ten Jagdgeschader (JG 1, 2, 3, 21, 26, 27, 51, 53, 54 and 77) had approximately 1,000 Bf 109E fighters on strength. The remaining C- and D-series aircraft now served as training aircraft or in limited numbers in the night fighter role.

Deliveries of the Bf 109E-4, equipped with improved MG FF cannon and the now production-ready MG FF/M engine-mounted weapon, began in early 1940. A trials unit under the command of Hauptmann W. Rubensdörfer, Erprobungsgruppe 210, began operations with the Bf 109E-4 in the fighter-bomber role in the subsequent campaign against France. Equipped with an ETC 500 stores rack, the fighter-bomber version was designated the Bf 109E-4/B. In July 1940, 3/EGr 210 operated aircraft of this type from bases on the Channel Coast. Results were favorable and each Jagdgeschwader received instructions to form its own Jabo-Staffel (Jabo = Jagdbomber or fighter-bomber).

The Bf 109E-4 also demonstrated its ability as a fighter aircraft over England. The RAF lost 631 Hurricanes and 403 Spitfires in the period from mid-July until the end of October. The Luftwaffe's fighter losses in the same period were 610 Bf 109s and 235 Bf 110s.

The Bf 109E-5 was a tactical reconnaissance aircraft based on the E-4 series. The wing-mounted cannon armament was deleted and a RB 21/18 aerial mapping camera was installed in the fuselage. The Bf 109E-6 was also a tactical reconnaissance aircraft powered by a DB 601 N instead of a DB 601 A in-line engine. The Bf 109E-7, a "fighter with increased range," followed in summer 1940. It was virtually identical to the Bf 109E-4/B, and a fuselage stores rack for the carriage of a 300-liter auxiliary fuel tank or bombs was installed as standard equipment. The same applied to the Bf 109E-8 single-seat fighter, whose airframe was similar to that of the Bf 109E-7. Converted Bf 109E-7/N (DB 601 N) fighters equipped with a Rb 50/30 camera in the fuselage for the reconnaissance role received the designation Bf 109E-9.

The standard German fighter maintained its superiority over the Balkans and in the early stages of Operation Barbarossa; however the need for improvement was recognized early on - not the case with other aircraft types. The Messerschmitt team in Augsburg began work on the Bf 109F, which was to be powered by the improved DB 601 E engine, in early 1940. Four E-series aircraft served as prototypes (V 21 to V 24), equipped with the new DB 601 E power plant as well as an experimental installation of an engine-mounted MG 151 cannon. The wing-mounted weapons were deleted. The future F-series was to include other new features as well: a propeller spinner of improved aerodynamic shape, a more streamlined engine cowling with improved oil cooler, and a larger rudder.

Bf 109E-1 of the Fieseler Factory Protection Staffel with Leutnant Riediger in the cockpit. The Staffel remained in existence from October 16, 1939 until August 7, 1940.

Above: Patrols were increased over the northwestern part of Germany to defend against incursions by enemy aircraft.

Final preparations before a mission over the Channel.

Below: A Bf 109E-1 of JG 2 photographed just prior to taking off on a mission in the west.

9

Forward airfield in France in the summer of 1940.

A Bf 109E between sorties on the Channel Coast. The unit is hosting a visitor from the Kriegsmarine.

This Bf 109E-4 was stationed at Rotterdam-Waalhaven. The aircraft was part of the Replacement and Training Staffel of JG 26.

Feldwebel Richtmann in front of his aircraft, which belonged to III/JG 27.

Left: Another aircraft of JG 26's Replacement and Training Staffel, which was based in the Netherlands.

Left:

The Bf 109E-3 was powered by a DB 601 Aa engine. Standard armament was two 7.9-mm MG 17 machine-guns and two 20-mm MG FF cannon.

Below: This Bf 109E-2 belonged to the Stab of JG 26. In the cockpit is the unmistakable figure of Adolf Galland. Note the telescopic sight mounted in the windscreen.

Above: The Bf 109E-4 saw wide service with the fighter units of the Luftwaffe and saw a great deal of action over Western Europe.

Right: A damaged propeller, the result of a forced landing after a successful mission over the Southwest England.

Bottom:
A Bf 109E-4 equipped with a rear-view mirror over the windscreen.

A Bf 109E-8 of III/JG 26 after a forced landing in Northern France.

An unidentified pilot of 10 (Jabo)/JG 27 in France in autumn 1941.

This Bf 109E-4 formed part of the equipment of the I/JG 3.

SKG 210 flew numerous fighter-bomber missions against targets in Southern England. Here one of the unit's aircraft, a Bf 109E-3/Bo, is seen parked at its dispersal.

Bf 109E of I/JG 52. The aircraft overturned while landing on a makeshift airfield in Russia.

II/JG 27 adopted the "Berlin Bear" as its emblem in 1940.

The aircraft of Hauptmann Rudolf Lochner of II/JG 53. The emblem is the coat of arms of the Munich Cooperative of the 1860's.

A Bf 109E-7 flown by JG 26's Replacement and Training Staffel in 1941.

Top Left:

Above left: The Bf 109T-2
fighters of 3/JG 77
operated from bases at
Lister, Herdla and
Vaernes. Depicted here is
"White 8."

Top Right:

Above: Leutnant Hondt of the
Jagdstaffel Helgoland sitting on the
cockpit sill of his aircraft, July 4, 1943.

Left: A Bf 109T-2 of 11/JG 11 in Norway.

The Bf 109T-2 was based mainly in Northern Germany, Denmark and Norway to defend against incursions by British aircraft.

The Bf 109T seen here (WerkNr. 7767) was flown by Oberleutnant Christmann of JG 11 from its base at Lister.

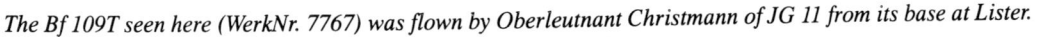

Due to difficulties associated the provision of engines (DB 601 E) and weapons (MG 151), the Bf 109F-1, deliveries of which commenced in the late autumn of 1940, was equipped with the DB 601 N and the MG FF/M as well as MG 17 machine-guns in the fuselage. At the same time, testing of the new series revealed a problem with vibration in the fuselage, which led to the crash of several aircraft. Following structural reinforcement of the airframe, it was not until March-April 1941 that JG 2 and JG 26 became the first operational units to receive the Bf 109F-1.

The MG 151 was first installed in the Bf 109F-2, deliveries of which began in April 1941. Otherwise the type differed little from the Bf 109F-1. The Bf 109F-3 saw a return to the armament of the Bf 109F-1; however the B 601 E power plant was installed. The Bf 109F-2 was delivered mainly to JG 2, 26, 27 and 53. JG 2 and JG 26 on the "Channel Front" received the bulk of the Bf 109F-3s in late 1941.

With the start of production of the Bf 109F-4, deliveries of the MG 151/20 and the DB 601 E were finally sufficient for series installation. Deliveries of this new Bf 109, the most advanced so far in terms of power plant and armament, began in 1942 to nearly every Luftwaffe unit and the type remained in front-line service well into 1943. In addition to numerous Rüstsätze (equipment kits), there existed versions for the fighter-bomber role (F-4/B), with tropical equipment (F-4/trop), and with GM-1 injection (F-4/Z). Also available to the Luftwaffe's long-range reconnaissance units were limited numbers of the Bf 109F-5 and F-6, which, for example, were operated by 1(F)/122 based in Sardinia.

The E-Stelle Rechlin tested the Fw 190 parallel to its work on the Bf 109. Progress was slow due to difficulties with the BMW 801 radial engine. In September 1941 one Gruppe of JG 26 received the Fw 190 A-1 for front-line testing. Success was limited due to recurring difficulties with the engines. A decision had to be made whether to continue quantity production of the Fw 190 at all; as a result the test station command was instructed to carry out comparative performance and handling tests involving the Fw 190 A-2 and Bf 109F-4 as quickly as possible. The following are extracts from the resulting report, which was issued on December 10, 1941:

"OBJECTIVES":
1. Comparison of the performance of both types paying special   attention to those aspects concerning front-line tactical use.
2. Assessment of the technical status of the Fw 190 A-2 based on   operational experience.
3. Proposals for changes.
4. General assessment of the aircraft with regard to the planned production program.

Re. 1:
(a) SPEED:
The Fw 190 A-2 is not quite as fast as the Bf 109F-4. The Fw's inferiority is most noticeable at higher altitudes where it is approximately 15 to 20 kph slower, while it is practically as fast between 4,000 and 4,500 meters. It is equally fast at ground level or even 10 kph faster.

(b) DIVING PERFORMANCE:
Tests revealed that the Fw 190 A-2 achieved a several hundred meter lead at all heights. The steeper and longer the dive, the greater this lead became.

(c) CLIMBING PERFORMANCE:
The Fw 190 A-2 is much inferior in the climb:

	Fw 190 A-2	Bf 109F-4
1,000 to 5,000 m	4 min 50 sec	4 min
5,000 to 10,000 m	18 min 30 sec	12 min 30 sec

The Fw 190 A-2's time to climb from 1,000 to 10,000 meters is thus 6 minutes longer. This represents an approximately 50% poorer performance.

(d) CONTROL FORCES, MANEUVERING:
The control forces of the Fw 190 A-2 are considered light. Unlike the Bf 109, even at 700 kph the aircraft can be maneuvered with bearable control forces. Maneuverability is good and its superiority over the Bf 109 in this aspect is especially noticeable in reversals and at high speeds. The Fw 190's rate of roll represents a significant advance which is very noticeable, especially in air combat.

Servicing the engine of a JG 26 Bf 109 at a base in Western Europe.

(e) TAKEOFF AND LANDING CHARACTERISTICS:

Takeoff by the Fw 190 A-2 is approximately 60 to 70 meters longer by virtue of its greater weight, for the same reason landing speed is approximately 15 kph higher. However, by virtue of the robust construction of its undercarriage and its stability even at low speeds (no tendency to drop a wing), it is possible to land the Fw 190 almost as short as the Bf 109. Too much or too little speed on landing results in a higher sink rate than is the case with the Bf 109, so that in one case the aircraft drops rapidly, in the other case the landing run is greatly increased. There is no tendency to

swing. It is especially noteworthy that belly landings resulted in no significant damage; in no case was there twisting of the wings or of the fuselage, which is almost always the case with the Bf 109. This has resulted in high aircraft losses in front-line units.

Re. 2:
(a) STRUCTURAL STRENGTH OF THE FW 190:

It is completely adequate for all operational demands. It is not expected that reinforcements will have to be carried out later as with the Bf 109.

(b) ENGINE FW 190

Based on previous experience, especially with JG 26, the engine must be characterized as unreliable and not yet ready for front-line service. The average operating period achieved in service has just reached the twenty-five hour mark. ...

Re. 3:
(e) COCKPIT:

The cockpit is rather narrow ... Cockpit ventilation must be significantly improved. ...

(h) ARMAMENT:

A request has been raised to be able to select the two wing cannon separately if desired when firing the centrally-mounted weapons....

Re. 4:

The following observations are offered concerning the existing ratio of production of the Fw 190 to the Bf 109:

At the present time the engine is so unreliable that the aircraft (Fw 190) is only conditionally suitable for operations. It cannot be assumed that a front-line-capable, air-cooled engine in the 2,000-HP range will come out in the distant future. The development of enemy aircraft will probably mean that we will have to resort to powerful liquid-cooled engines in spite of the great advantages offered by air-cooled. It is intended to install the DB 603, as the next liquid-cooled engine, in the Fw 190 after the BMW 801 D. The DB 603 is a completely new engine which will also have its teething troubles. Technical difficulties with the Fw 190 will therefore persist for a long time, while meanwhile the Bf 109F or G remains the sole fighter aircraft really suitable for front-line operations. It (the Fw 190) is just as unsafe to operate (due to engine failure) over Russia or other marine areas as in action over the Channel. The makeup of the pilot corps is no longer such that losses due to technical shortcomings can be accepted.

Development shows clearly that the Bf 109 will always remain faster than the Fw 190 and possess a better rate of climb. But the best climbing performance cannot be ignored. Even if that of the Fw 190 is adequate at the moment in the air war over the Channel, its inferiority when equipped with the BMW 801 C compared to the Bf 109F-4, with a 50% greater time to climb to 10,000 meters, cannot in any case be overlooked. It is estimated that with the BMW 801 D its inferiority will still be 25 to 30 percent of the climb performance of the Bf 109F-4.

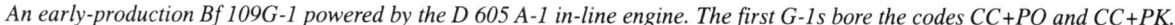

An early-production Bf 109G-1 powered by the D 605 A-1 in-line engine. The first G-1s bore the codes CC+PO and CC+PK.

Based on the considerations presented here the ratio of 50 % for the Fw 190 appears to be too high, even given the Bf 109's greater vulnerability to battle damage."

This report gave no definitive advantage to either aircraft. The Bf 109 had certain weaknesses - for example its narrow track landing gear, which was aggravated by the inexperience of the replacement pilots. The Bf 109 was also more fragile, but on the other hand it was clearly superior to the Fw 190 in rate of climb and performance at altitude. The Fw 190 was a heavier, more robust aircraft with a heavier armament, and over the course of time its power plant problems could be solved. For these reasons - and because aircraft were urgently needed - the Bf 109 and the Fw 190 remained standard equipment of the fighter and fighter-bomber units of the Luftwaffe until the end of the war.

Bf 109F VARIANTS

F-1/B	Fighter-bomber with stores rack
F-1/trop	Fighter aircraft with equipment kit for desert operations
F-2/B	Fighter-bomber with ETC 250 stores rack
F-2/trop	Fighter aircraft with equipment kit for desert operations
F-2/Z	Fighter aircraft with GM-1 (nitrous-oxide) injection, larger supercharger air intake, revised oil cooler and new propeller
F-4/B	Fighter-bomber with ETC 250 stores rack
F-4/trop	Fighter aircraft with equipment kit for desert operations
F-4/Z	Fighter aircraft with GM-1 injection, larger supercharger air intake, revised oil cooler and new propeller
F-4/R1	Fighter aircraft with one MG 151/20 beneath each wing
F-4/R2	Tactical reconnaissance aircraft with Rb 20x30 camera, no radio
F-4/R3	Tactical reconnaissance aircraft with Rb 50x30 camera, no radio
F-4/R4	Tactical reconnaissance aircraft with Rb 75x30 camera, no radio
F-4/R8	Tactical reconnaissance aircraft with Rb 75x30 camera, with radio

With the appearance of the G-series, which was powered by the DB 605 engine, Bf 109 development reached a temporary high point. A number of important features had to be taken into consideration before design work on the high-altitude fighter began:
- use of the new, more powerful DB 605 engine
- standard installation of fittings on the fuselage and wings for the carriage of diverse external loads, in order to be able to create a combat aircraft capable of performing the widest variety of roles as quickly as possible under front-line conditions. To achieve this, six equipment kits were initially planned:
R1: ETC 900/IXb for 1 x 250-kg store
R2: ETC 50/VIIb for 4 x 50-kg stores

Servicing the first Bf 109G delivered to JG 26.

A Bf 109F-4 of JG 51's 4th Staffel.

Funeral service for a member of III/JG 2 with band and honor guard.

Crash landing by an aircraft of IV/JG 1.

The aircraft of the Gruppenkommandeur of II/JG 52. Although the machine has a cockpit canopy from an early Bf 109E, the fuel triangle beneath the cockpit and the arrangement of the wing flaps clearly identifies it as a Bf 109F.

R3: 300-liter drop tank
R5: MK 108 cannon in gondolas beneath the wings
R6: MG 151/20 cannon in gondolas beneath the wings
R7: direction finder (DF) with antenna
- pressurized cockpit
- standard back and head armor
- strengthened wing
- fittings for subsequent installation of a GM-1 system
- roller-mounted wing slats and enlarged oil cooler

Testing of three Bf 109G-0 machines (WerkNr. 14001-14003, VJ+WA to VJ+WC) powered by the DB 601 E began in autumn 1941. The new DB 605 became available with the Bf 109G-1. This variant had a pressurized cockpit as well as a strengthened wing and most went into service as high-altitude fighters with 11/JG 1 and 11/JG 26 in late 1942. Beginning in 1943 both units also began receiving the Bf 109G-3 which had different radio equipment (FuG 16Z) as well as a strengthened fuselage and wing.

The Bf 109G-2 saw service in large numbers with JG 2, JG 3, JG 5, JG 27, JG 51, JG 52, JG 53, JG 54, JG 77 and Jagdgruppen Ost and West. The airframe of the G-2 was similar to that of the Bf 109G-1 but it lacked the latter's GM-1 injection system and pressurized cockpit. The Bf 109G-2/R2 reconnaissance version was used by 2 (H)/Aufklärungsgruppe 14, NAG 2 and one Staffel each of FAG 122 and 123.

Also built in significant numbers, the Bf 109G-4 began reaching the front-line units in November 1942. This series was developed from the G-2 and in addition to the FuG 16Z it had a reinforced wing and fuselage to permit the use of further equipment kits.

The first Bf 109Gs underwent extensive testing at the E-Stelle Rechlin.

A word about equipment kits (Rüstsätze). These were often combined, a common example being R3 and R6 (fuselage drop tank and MG 151/20 beneath the wings). The "trop" suffix was added to the designations of aircraft fitted with tropical equipment (sand filter, survival kit, cockpit sun umbrella). In some cases conversions or modifications also resulted in the use of the "R" suffix. The G-4 series offers one such example; in one case R4 stood for a fighter-bomber variant used in small numbers, while it was also used to designate the reconnaissance version equipped with a Rb 50/30 camera. Some Rüstsätze changed in the course of the war or were redesignated by the manufacturer, adding to the confusion and making source material contradictory.

The Bf 109G-5, which was equipped with a pressurized cockpit and MG 131 machine-guns in place of the MG 17s of earlier versions, was followed by the Bf 109G-6. This major production variant began reaching the fighter units in February 1943 and was to become the backbone of the German air defense. The most significant difference between the G-6, which remained in production until the summer of 1944, and its predecessor the G-4, was the installation of two MG 131 heavy machine-guns in the fuselage in place of the smaller-caliber MG 17. Bulged fairings were necessary to cover the revised ammunition feeds and these became an identifying feature of the type. The Bf 109G-6 also saw the introduction of the so-called "Galland-Panzer" head armor and soon afterward of the "Erla-Haube" hood for improved visibility from the cockpit. As well a larger fin and rudder was introduced into series production beginning in the spring of 1944. There were numerous converted variants of the G-6, identifiable by the "U" suffix.

The Bf 109G-5 was the last of the series to be built with a pressurized cockpit and thereafter all variants were assigned an even number. Thus there was no Bf 109G-7. The G-8 was a tactical reconnaissance version of the Bf 109G-6 with DF equipment and a revised arrangement of fuselage cameras. The aircraft served with NAG 5, NAG 8, NAG 15, AufklGr 14 and the Finnish Air Force.

Beginning in late summer 1944, older G-series aircraft, mostly G-6s and G-14s, underwent a conversion process intended to bring them up to Bf 109K-4 standard, resulting in the Bf 109G-10. The majority were issued to JG 2, JG 3, JG4, JG 6, JG 27, JG 77 and JG 300, as well as to II/NJG 11, I/KG(J) 6 and in limited numbers to NAG 2, NAG4, NAG 14 and NAG 15. The G-10 remained in production alongside the K-4 until shortly before the end of the war.

In early 1944 approximately 145 Bf 109G-2, G-3, G-4 and G-6 airframes were converted into G-12 two-seat training aircraft in response to the high accident rate being experienced in conversion to the Bf 109 - caused by drastically abbreviated pilot training and in part by the Bf 109's narrow track undercarriage.

The Bf 109G-14 was a "mongrel series" resulting from the urgent demands of the air war. This final production version of the Bf 109G was integrated smoothly into the final stages of G-6 production and was also built alongside the G-10 and K-4. The first Bf 109G-14 fighters reached JG 4, JG 76 and JG 77 in France in June 1944. Later almost every Jagdgeschwader, those bomber units in the process of converting to fighters (KG 6, KG 27 and KG 55), elements of II and III/NJG 11, and the tactical reconnaissance units NAG 1 to 4 and NAG 14 received the type.

The Bf 109G was also flown by units of the Italian Air Force. In a report on the status of the Italian flying units dated March 22, 1945, the Commanding General of the German Luftwaffe in Italy described the Italian fighter units as follows:

Bf 109G-2 fighters of the Stab of JG 51 in the USSR in 1942.

"Ist Italian Fighter Group

1st Squadron in Gallarate, the transfer of remaining elements (formerly at Lonate-Pozzolo) to Gallarate has been ordered and is being carried out, pilot complement 58; on hand in Holzkirchen: 42 Bf 109G-10 and G-14, 3 K-4. Operational since 10/3/1945. Personnel strength 591.

IInd Italian Fighter Group

Headquarters, 4th and 6th Squadrons in Aviano, 5th Squadron in Osoppo, pilot complement 43; aircraft complement: 16 Bf 109G-6, 30 Bf 109G-10 and G-14, operational since 19/10/1944. Personnel strength: 585.

IIIrd Italian Fighter Group

Flying personnel and senior technical personnel in Holzkirchen for conversion and indoctrination. Remaining surface elements in Deso near Milan, pilot complement: 78, aircraft complement: 10 Bf 109G-6, 2 G-10, 2 G-12, 2 G-14, 4 Me 108, 1 Kl 35, personnel strength 541."

BF 109G VARIANTS

G-1/trop	Fighter aircraft with equipment for desert operations
G-1/R1	Fighter aircraft with no stores rack
G-1/R2	Reconnaissance aircraft with Rb 50/30, no engine cannon, drop tank, some equipped with GM-1 system
	Fighter aircraft with 300-liter drop tank
	Fighter aircraft with MG 151/20 in underwing gondolas
G-2/trop	Equipped for desert operations
G-2/R1	Fighter-bomber with ETC 500/IXb and jettisonable extra undercarriage leg
G-2/R2	Reconnaissance aircraft with GM-1 injection and camera equipment (choice of 5x30, 50x30, 20x30 or 12.5/7x9 systems)

This Bf 109G-2 belonged to the II/JG 54 Grünherz (Green Heart).

A Bf 109G-2 of JG 52 during preparations for takeoff.

G-2/R3	Fighter aircraft with 300-liter drop tank for increased range	G-4/R6	Fighter aircraft with MG 151/20 cannon beneath the wings
	Reconnaissance aircraft with camera equipment, GM-1 injection	G-4/R7	Fighter aircraft with DF equipment (limited numbers)
G-2/R6	Fighter aircraft with MG 151/20 cannon beneath the wings	G-5/AS	Fighter aircraft with DB 605 AS with GM-1 and two fuselage-mounted MG 131 machine-guns
G-2/U2	Fighter aircraft with Me P6 braking propeller		
G-3/trop	Fighter aircraft with equipment for desert operations	G-5/trop	Fighter aircraft with equipment for desert operations
G-3/R1	Fighter-bomber with ETC 500/Ib	G-5/R1	Fighter-bomber with ETC 500/IXb
G-3/R2	Fighter aircraft with GM-1 system	G-5/R2	Reconnaissance aircraft with DB 605 A-1 and GM-1 system
G-3/R3	Extended range fighter with 300-liter drop tank	G-5/R2/AS	Reconnaissance aircraft with DB 605 AS and GM-1
G-3/R6	Fighter aircraft with MG 151/20 cannon beneath the wings	G-5/R3	Reconnaissance aircraft with 300-liter drop tank, Rb 40/30 to be replaced by Rb 50/30
G-4/trop	Fighter aircraft with equipment for desert operations	G-5/R4	Reconnaissance aircraft with Rb 50/30, no MG 17s
G-4/R1	Fighter-bomber with ETC 500/IXb	G-5/R6	Fighter aircraft with MG 151/20 cannon beneath the wings
G-4/R2	Fighter-bomber with ETC 50/VIIb (limited numbers)	G-5/R7	Reconnaissance aircraft with DF equipment
G-4/R2	Reconnaissance aircraft with Rb 50/30, no engine cannon	G-5/U2	High-altitude fighter with DB 605 A-1 and GM-1
G-4/R3	Long-range fighter with 300-liter drop tank	G-5/U2/AS	High-altitude fighter with DB 605 AS with GM-1 system
G-4/R4	Reconnaissance version with MG 17 machine-guns deleted (unit-level conversion)		

The Kommodore of JG 52 in the cockpit of his Bf 109G-2 during the Russian campaign.

G-6/AS	Fighter aircraft with DB 605 AS with GM-1 system	G-8/R7	Reconnaissance aircraft with DF equipment (installed on production line)
G-6/trop	Fighter aircraft with equipment for desert operations	G-8/U2	Fighter aircraft, unit-level conversion to MW 50 system using GM-equipment
G-6/N	Night fighter	G-8/U3	Fighter aircraft with MW 50 injection (unit-level conversion)
G-6/R1	Fighter-bomber with ETC 500 IXb		
G-6/R2	Fighter with MW 50 injection	G-10/AS	Fighter aircraft with DB 605 AS and revised engine cowling
G-6/R3	Reconnaissance aircraft with Rb 75/30 and drop tank	G-10/R1	Fighter-bomber with ETC 500 IXb
G-6/R4	Reconnaissance aircraft with Rb 50/30	G-10/R2	Tactical reconnaissance aircraft with Rb 50/30 camera, MW 50 injection
G-6/R4/AS	Reconnaissance aircraft with GM-1 system and DB 605 AS	G-10/R3	Fighter aircraft with 300-liter drop tank
G-6/R6	Fighter aircraft with MG 151/20 cannon beneath the wings	G-10/R5	Reconnaissance aircraft with Rb 12.5/7x9 camera
G-6/U2	Version retrofitted with GM-1 system	G-10/R6	Fighter aircraft with MG 151/20 cannon beneath the wings
G-6/U3	Version retrofitted with MW 50 system	G-10/R7	Fighter aircraft with rocket-launching tubes (210-mm)
G-6/U4	Fighter aircraft converted to accept MK 108/M engine cannon	G-10/U4	Fighter aircraft with MK 108 engine-mounted cannon and MW 50 injection
G-8/R1	Fighter-bomber with ETC 500 IXb	G-14/AS	Fighter aircraft with DB 605 AS, revised engine cowling and MW 50 system
G-8/R2	Reconnaissance aircraft with one Rb 50/30 camera		
G-8/R3	Reconnaissance aircraft with two Rb 32/7x9 cameras	G-14/R1	Fighter-bomber with ETC 500/IXb
G-8/R5	Reconnaissance aircraft with two Rb 12.5/7x9 cameras, MG 151/20 deleted	G-14/R2	Tactical reconnaissance aircraft with Rb 50/30 camera and MW 50 system
G-8/R6	Fighter aircraft with MG 151/20 cannon beneath the wings	G-14/R3	Fighter aircraft with 300-liter drop tank for increased range

This Bf 109G-2 (WerkNr. 14513) of 3/JG 3 was built by WNF (Messerschmitt's Wiener-Neustadt factory).

This Bf 109 was flown for a time by the ace Johannes Trautloft.

Right: A B 109G-4 with an experimental installation of three gondola-mounted MG 151/20 cannon. This arrangement was not adopted for service use.

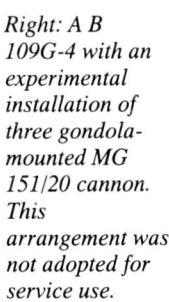

4 (Fernauflärung)/ 123, a long-range reconnaissance unit, flew several Bf 109G-4s with fixed armament removed on missions over Western Europe.

30

*Above: Bf 109G-6
of JG 54
photographed soon
after delivery to the
unit.*

*Right: Installing a film cassette
in a well-camouflaged Bf
109G-4 of 4 (F)/123.*

This photo was taken on the
Eastern Front in the winter of
1942/43. The Bf 109G
belonged to one of the
Spanish volunteer Staffeln.

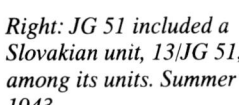

Right: JG 51 included a
Slovakian unit, 13/JG 51,
among its units. Summer
1943.

Servicing a Bf 109G on
a rear-area base on the
southern sector of the
Eastern Front.

This Bf 109G-6/trop of JGr. 50 was equipped with two launching tubes for WGr.21 air-to-air rockets.

The Wiener-Neustadt factory built the Bf 109G-6, G-6/R3 and G-6/R4. The production block began with the number 200.

A parked Bf 109G of III/JG 3, which was stationed in Army Group South's zone of operations.

Servicing a Bf 109G under field conditions.

Pilots of 9/JG 77 photographed in Southern Italy in the summer of 1943. The aircraft is a Bf 109G-6/R6.

Right: This Bf 109G-6 belonged to 1/JGr. 50, based at Wiesbaden-Erbenheim in the summer of 1943. Sitting in front of the aircraft is Oberleutnant Grislawski.

Center: This experimental paint scheme, which was devised by JG 77 Herzas (Ace of Hearts), was intended to disrupt the aim of enemy gunners.

A Bf 109G-6 of JG 3 armed with two rocket-launching tubes waits the next mission.

Acceptance flight at a Messerschmitt factory in Southern Germany. The aircraft is a Bf 109G-6.

This photograph of Leutnant Hanf of III/JG 77 and a friend sitting on the wing of his aircraft was taken in July 1943.

Leutnant Gerhard Hanf on his Bf 109G in Southern Italy.

Above and below: Acceptance flights in progress at the Augsburg or Regensburg factory. The factory-fresh aircraft are the Bf 109G-6/ R6 variant.

This Bf 109G-6 was photographed at Veszprem, Hungary while being ferried to the Eastern Front in 1943.

Another view of the aircraft. Bearing the code VN+PR, it is a Bf 109G-6/R6 with gondola-mounted MG 151/20 cannon.

G-14/R6	Fighter aircraft with MG 151/20 cannon beneath the wings and MW 50 system
G-14/U4	Conversion with engine-mounted MK 108 cannon and MW 50 injection

The Bf 109K represented an attempt on the part of the RLM to counter the growing raw materials shortage. In addition to a more powerful engine (DB 605 D), the type was to make use of readily available materials in its construction, especially wood. The Wolf Hirth GmbH of Nabern/Teck constructed a prototype wooden wing. In the end, however, quantity production failed to come about as the design was too expensive and there were technical problems as well. The designers then focussed their efforts on at least combining all the previous changes of the Bf 109G-10 and G-14 in a new series.

By October 1943 a Bf 109K mockup was ready for inspection at Messerschmitt's Wiener-Neustadt factory. Plans to begin production of the Bf 109K-1, which included a pressurized cockpit and MK 108 armament, in July 1944 were quickly frustrated by the drastically deteriorating military situation.

At least one prototype of the Bf 109K-2 equipped with a MK 108 engine-mounted cannon was tested at Tarnewitz in autumn 1944. On the other hand the Bf 109K-3, a high-altitude fighter with a pressurized cockpit and GM-1 system, was never built.

Following the completion of flight testing, toward the end of October 1944 the first of approximately 700 Bf 109K-4s to be built were delivered to III/JG 27. Deliveries followed soon afterward to the IVth Gruppe of the same Geschwader as well as to III/JG 4 and III/

JG 77. JG 6 also received the Bf 109K-4. The Geschwader submitted a report describing its experiences with the Bf 109K-4 in front-line service:

"TECHNICAL EXPERIENCES

Bf 109
I. Airframe

Newly-delivered aircraft are very trouble-prone in the first 5-10 flying hours. The complaints are almost always the same and these place a great technical burden on the unit and reduce operational readiness. Complaints of the following nature turn up almost on a regular basis:

- play in the elevator-horizontal stabilizer hinges
- loose spacers on the elevator control cables
- excessively-long attachment bolts on the undercarriage leg suspension fitting
- leaking or plugged methanol system
- faulty wiring in the electrical system
- loose and improperly installed spark plugs
- oiling of the engines due to flanges developing leaks
- poorly adjusted weapons
- aircraft radio equipment unserviceable, especially radio sets

II. Engine

One Bf 109K-4 was forced to make an emergency landing due to engine failure. Investigation revealed water in the fuel system. Similar discoveries were made in other aircraft of the series.

Close-up view of the Bf 109G-6/R6 of Oberfeldwebel Heinrich Bartels (IV/JG 27) at a Sicilian air base in the summer of 1943.

Cause:

The methanol system installed to provide increased range may be set to "fuel" or "methanol" by means of a lever. This lever is now most usually activated unintentionally. Damage like that described above is the result if the tank is filled with a methanol-water mixture. Simply locking the lever would prevent this.

III. Weapons System

(1) When the MK 108 is used the weapon fails after firing a few shots. The cause was determined to be the insulating material of the round's firing cap, which springs out and lodges itself in the bore hole of the steel bushing for the firing pin. A certain amount of cleaning of the breechblock is necessary after each flight in which the guns are fired, but this must be seen only as an interim solution.

(2) Several failures to fire were caused by firing pins striking the ammunition off-center. The firing pins were replaced rather than cleaned.

(3) On several aircraft the ammunition feed (MK 108) was misaligned with the weapon by 3-5 cm. The result was that the belt could not be fed properly.

(4) Feeding the belt into the MK 108 in the Bf 109K-4 runs into difficulties and takes a great deal of time. In order to allow faster feeding of the belt feed band, headquarters installed an access cover on the bottom side of the spent shell casing chute. This made possible good control of the ammunition being fed into the weapon and eliminated feed difficulties.

(5) Only some of the aircraft are outfitted with fusing selector boxes and fusing battery boxes.

IV. Procurement of Replacement Parts

There are difficulties in the procurement of the Fl 8/2926 E-5AD tall tailwheel, the fusing battery box and the fusing selector box. Other difficult to obtain parts were removed from aircraft which have been written off."

The Bf 109K-6 represented another improvement in armament. It was proposed that this "Sturmjäger" (assault fighter) be armed with a MK 108 engine cannon, two MG 131 machine-guns mounted in the fuselage and two MK 108 cannon in the wings. MW 50 injection was to be standard equipment. Powered by a DB 605 ASCM/DCM engine, it was calculated that this most potent Bf 109 would attain a speed of 728 kph at a height of 8,000 meters. The sole prototype was rolled out at Regensburg in December 1944 and was then ferried to Tarnewitz for weapons tests.

All other versions of the K-series (Bf 109K-8, K-10, K-12 and K-14) progressed no farther than the drawing board. There were no uneven designations after the Bf 109K-4.

A Bf 109G-6 of JG 27 photographed prior to takeoff. The aircraft is equipped with a 300-liter drop tank.

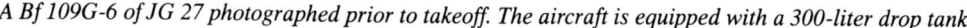

In anticipation of quantity production of the Bf 109K-6, the OKL released for distribution a plan titled "Aircraft Equipment of the Fighter Wings" dated February 4, 1945.

"(1) To the degree that aircraft production allows, the equipping of fighter wings with one type is to be strived for in the course of the rationalization of the equipment of fighter wings.

(2) The planned equipment of the fighter wings is as follows:

Instructing ground personnel of JG 27 in the servicing of the Bf 109.

Takeoff clearance for aircraft of JG 102. The majority of the unit's machines were the Bf 109G-6 and G-14 variants.

41

UNIT	PRESENT EQUIPMENT	PLANNED AIRCRAFT EQUIPMENT FOR THE ACHIEVEMENT OF HOMOGENEITY
JG 1	2 gr. Fw 190 A-8/A-9 1 Gr. Bf 109G-14/AS	He 162 Conversion order for I/JG 1 and formation order for Stabsstaffel JG 1 already issued
JG 3	3 Gr. Bf 109K-4/G-10 1 Gr. Fw 190 (Sturm)	unchanged Bf 109K-6 (Sturm)
JG 4	3 Gr. Bf 109K-4/G-10 1 Gr. Fw 190 (Sturm)	unchanged Bf 109K-6 (Sturm)
JG 6	2 Gr. Fw 190 A-8/A-9 1 Gr. Bf 109G-14/AS	unchanged Fw 190 D
JG 7	2 Gr. Me 262	unchanged, with incorporation of JG 54, to be redesignated II/JG 7
JG 11	2 Gr. Fw 190 A-8/A-9 1 Gr. Bf 109K-4/G-10	unchanged Fw 190 D-11/D-12/D-13
JG 26 including III/JG 54	4 Gr. Fw 190 D-9	unchanged, with IV/JG 26 incorporated as III/ JG 54
JG 54	3 Gr. Fw 190 A-8/A-9	unchanged, with II/ZG 76 incorporated as III/JG 54
JG 300	3 Gr. Bf 109G-10/R6 1 Gr. Fw 190 (Sturm)	unchanged Bf 109K-6 (Sturm)
JG 301	3 Gr. Fw 190 D-11 1 Gr. Bf 109G-10/R6	Ta 152 H Order for conversion of III/JG 301 and formation of Stabsstaffel JG 301 already issued

IXth Flying Corps (Fighter)

UNIT	PRESENT EQUIPMENT	PLANNED
KG(J) 27	2 Gr. Bf 109G-10/R6, K-4 1 Gr. Fw 190 A-9/R11	unchanged Conversion to Bf 109G-10/R6 without withdrawal from operations planned
KG(J) 6	2 Gr. Bf 109G-10/R6, K-4 1 Gr. with no aircraft	unchanged Conversion of III/KG(J) 6 to the Me 262 planned after JG 7 and KG(J) 54
KG(J) 54	3 Gr. Me 262	unchanged planned for later
KG(J) 55	3 Gr. Me 262	unchanged
KG(J) 30	3 Gr. Bf 109K-4/R6	unchanged

This Bf 109G-6 was flown by Nahaufkläungs-gruppe (Tactical Reconnaissance Group) Blomberg shortly before the end of the war. The aircraft wears a "Red 4" in addition to the code N5+DK.

The remaining fighter units have already achieved homogeneity of aircraft equipment."

Only six weeks later there followed a realistic reassessment of the situation. In a letter dated March 20, 1945 the OKL - General der Jagdflieger, Gruppe Qu. - declared:

"The development in the equipment status of day fighter units is based on the standard types laid down in the emergency program and anticipates:

for Bf 109 units	K-4
for Fw 190 units	D-9, D-12 with change over to Ta 152 H and C

The arrival of the Ta 152 and its assignment to Fw 190 units will result in an improvement in the equipment status of these units.

Essentially Bf 109 development will conclude with the K-4 and will inevitably lead to the conversion of Bf 109 units - those not scheduled for disbandment - to TL (jet fighters, the author). Homogeneity of equipment is to be strived for, combination of similar types is temporary and to be accepted based on levels of production."

The proposed equipment changes for those units equipped with the Bf 109 thus looked as follows:

UNIT	PRESENT EQUIPMENT	CONVERT TO
III/JG 1	Bf 109G-10	He 162 (April-May)
II/JG	Bf 109G-10	K-4 when deliveries permit
III/JG 3	Bf 109K-4	unchanged
III/JG 4	Bf 109K-4	unchanged
IV/JG 4	Bf 109G-10	K-4
III/JG 5	Bf 109G-14	K-4 when deliveries permit
IV/JG 5	Bf 109G-14	K-4 when deliveries permit
III/JG 6	Bf 109G-14/AS	K-4 when deliveries permit
II/JG 11	Bf 109G-10	K-4 when deliveries permit
I/JG 27	Bf 109K-4	unchanged, 1.988 boost pressure increase
II/JG 27	Bf 109G-10	K-4 when deliveries permit
III/JG 27	Bf 109G-10	unchanged, 1.98 boost pressure increase
I/JG 51	Bf 109G-14	K-4 when deliveries permit
III/JG 51	Bf 109G-14	K-4 when deliveries permit
IV/JG 51	Bf 109G-14	K-4 when deliveries permit
I/JG 52	Bf 109G-14	K-4 when deliveries permit
II/JG 52	Bf 109G-14/U4	K-4 when deliveries permit
III/JG 52	Bf 109G-14	K-4 when deliveries permit
II/JG 53	Bf 109K-4	unchanged
III/JG 53	Bf 109K-4	unchanged, 1.98 boost pressure increase
IV/J 53	Bf 109K-4	unchanged, 1.98 boost pressure increase
I/JG 77	Bf 109G-14/U4	K4 when deliveries permit
II/JG 77	Bf 109G-10	K-4 when deliveries permit
III/JG 77	Bf 109G-10	K-4 when deliveries permit
III/JG 300	Bf 109G-10/ R6 via K-4 to Me 262	planned, deadline

This Bf 109G-6 belonged to an unidentified replacement and training Gruppe.

"White 8," a Bf 109G-6 of 1/JG 27, photographed in early 1944.

Bf 109G-6 of 8/JG 53 photographed at Bad Lippspringe during an intermediate stop in July 1944.

Unteroffizier Girnth of 8/JG 53 in front of his Bf 109G-6, which is equipped with a FuG 16 ZY.

44

IV/JG 300	Bf 109G-10 /R6 via K-4/R6 to Me 262	unknown	
I/KG(J) 6	Bf 109G-10/R6	K-4/R6 when deliveries permit	
II/KG(J) 6	Bf 109K-4	K-4/R6 when deliveries permit	
I/KG(J) 27	Bf 109G-10/R6	K-4/R6 when deliveries permit	
I/KG(J) 55	Bf 109G-10/R6		
II/KG(J) 55	Bf 109K-4	to industrial defense	
Ist Italian Fighter Group	Bf 109G-10 K-4	when deliveries permit	
IInd Italian Fighter Group	Bf 109G-10 K-4	when deliveries permit	
IIIrd Italian Fighter Group	Bf 109G-10 K-4	when deliveries permit	

The operational reports submitted by the air fleets provide an excellent insight into the actual strengths of the units equipped with the Bf 109. Toward the end of the war these numbers varied sharply according to the circumstances but they nevertheless reveal trends. According to a report by Luftflotte 6, on February 1, 1945 III/JG 1 had 27 Bf 109G-10s and G-14s, I/JG 3 16 Bf 109G-10s and G-14s. The IIIrd Gruppe of that Geschwader had 22 Bf 109K-4s on strength. I and IV/ JG 4 had 16 and 27 Bf 109G-10s respectively, while the IIIrd Gruppe had eight serviceable Bf 109K-4s. III/JG 11 had 37 Bf 109G-10s and G-14s, Stab/JG 51 two Bf 109G-10s, while the Ist Gruppe of the Geschwader had 25 serviceable Bf 109G-14s and III and IV/JG 51 five and thirty Bf 109G-6s and G-10s respectively. Stab/JG 52 had five serviceable Bf 109G-6s and G-10s, the Ist Gruppe 22 Bf 109G-10s and G-14s, and the IIrd Gruppe

25 Bf 109G-10s and G-14s. JG 77's strength report read: Ist Gruppe 18 Bf 109G-10s and G-14s, IInd Gruppe 10 Bf 109G-10s and IIIrd Gruppe eleven Bf 109K-4s. On the strength of IV(Erg.)/JG 1 were 54 Bf 109G-6s. Furthermore, I/NJG 5 and I/NJG 100 were equipped with the Bf 109G-14. The Bf 109G was also being used operationally the Stab and the first two Staffeln of NAG 2, NAG 3, NAG 4 and NAG 8 as well as 1.NAG 15.

A report by Luftflotte 6 submitted on March 21, 1945 revealed the authorized and actual strengths of those units equipped with the Bf 109:

UNIT	TYPE	AUTHORIZED	ACTUAL
III/JG 1	G/K	68	63
I/JG 3	G-10/G-14	38	38
II/JG 3	G-10/G-14	52	51
III/JG 3	G/K	40	39
III/JG 44tb	G/K	43	40
IV/JG 4	G-10/G-14	44	42
III/JG 6	G/K	32	23
II/JG 11	G/K	44	42
Stab JG 51	G-10	6	6
I/JG 51	G-14	55	32
III/JG 51	G-14	56	26
IV/JG 51	G-6/G-10	20	16
IV(Erg.)JG 1	no report		
Stab/JG 52	G/K-4	6	5
I/JG 52	G/K	37	26
III/JG 52	G/K	37	35
Stab/JG 77	G-14	3	3
I/JG 77	G/K	40	29
II/JG 77	G-10/G-14	43	36
III/JG 77	K-4	34	22
Stab/NAG 2	G	4	1

This abandoned Bf 109G was found at Prague-Ruzyne airfield at the end of the war.

1/NAG 2	G4tb	15	9
2/NAG 2	G4tb	6	4
Stab/NAG 3	G4tb	2	1
1/NAG 3	G-6/G-14	12	10
2/NAG 3	G G	9	6
Stab/NAG 4	G	in process of transfer	
1/NAG 4	G	13	9
Stab/NAG 8	G 4tb	4	
1/NAG 88	G-8/G-14	19	5
2/NAG 8	G	11	8
1/NAG 15	G-6/G-14	2	2

On April 26, 1945 Luftwaffe Command West reported 2/NAG 13 with four Bf 109G-6s and G-10s and the 3rd Staffel with no aircraft, III and IV/JG 53 with twelve Bf 109Gs and Ks each, III/JG 300 with 28 Bf 109Gs and Ks, I/NJG 11 with six Bf 109s, and 17/NJG 1 with twenty serviceable Bf 109G-6s. At that time II/JG 53 released its Bf 109G-6s to the General in Command of Fighters. At the same time Luftwaffe Command 4 reported II/JG 52 with 54 serviceable Bf 109s, Stab/NAG 14 with two, 2 and 3/NAG 14 with four and five Bf 109s respectively, and 13/NAG 12 with twelve Bf 109s. Stab/NAG 12 and the 2nd Staffel had a total of twenty aircraft (Bf 109 and Hs 126) ready for action. Fuel was in short supply everywhere, however, and the number of flights was severely restricted.

BF 109K VARIANTS

K-1 Planned replacement for the G-5 high-altitude fighter, pressurized cockpit, MK 108 armament, mockup only, completed by WNF in October 1943

K-2 Replacement for G-6/U4, one prototype (WerkNr. 600056) tested

K-3 Fighter with pressurized cockpit and improved high-altitude performance, project only

K-4 Production version with DB 605 D, two MG 131s in fuselage, MK 108 engine cannon

K-4/R1 Fighter-bomber with ETC 500/IXb or Installation Lock 503

K-4/R2 Tactical reconnaissance aircraft, MW 50 injection

K-4/R3 Fighter aircraft with Installation Lock 503 for jettisonable 300-liter auxiliary fuel tank

K-4/R4 Heavy fighter with MG 151/20 canon in underwing gondolas with 135 rounds per gun

K-4/R5 Reconnaissance aircraft with one 32/7x9 or two Rb 12.5/7x9 cameras

K-4/R6 Fighter aircraft with GM-1 system, BSK 16 gun camera activated when weapons fired

K-6 Fighter aircraft with two MG 131s in fuselage, MK 108 engine cannon, one MK 108 in each wing, one prototype built

K-8 Reconnaissance aircraft with DB 605 AS or DB 605 DCM, Rb 50/30 camera (project)

K-10 Fighter aircraft with MK 103 cannon instead of MK 108, project cancelled on account of lack of suitable cannon mount and excessive cost of conversion

K-12 Two-seat training aircraft (project)

K-14 High-performance fighter with DB 605 L and four-bladed propeller, under development at beginning of 1945

Several other Bf 109 developments are worthy of mention. One is the conversion of a number of Bf 109E-3s for use as carrier-based fighters from the aircraft carrier Zeppelin. An arrestor cable hook and catapult fittings were installed on a strengthened fuselage. The aircraft's wings, which folded for storage aboard the carrier, were increased in span. The aircraft was in fact put into production as the Bf 109T-1; however they were later converted back to land-based fighters as the Bf 109T-2.

The Bf 109H was a special high-altitude version with extended wings. A prototype was built in 1943. The projected production version was to be powered by the DB 605 or DB 628 engine.

The Bf 109Z was a proposed high-speed bomber and heavy fighter. One prototype was built in 1942/43 but was never flown. This rather curious aircraft consisted of two Bf 109F fuselages attached at the wings.

An early-model Bf 109G-10 seen in May 1945 after its capture by American troops.

The Bf 109 soldiered on in service with various air forces after the end of the war (Israel, Switzerland, Spain and Czechoslovakia) and in some cases production continued with alternative power plants (for example, as the Avia S-99).

The Bf 109G-12 trainer was the result of conversions of Bf 109G-2, G-3, G-4 and G-6 airframes.

Below: This Bf 109G-12 two-seater belonged to JG 101.

Below: This Bf 109G-6 was left behind on an abandoned airfield, probably because of a lack of spare parts or fuel.

SPECIFICATIONS OF THE MAIN VERSIONS OF THE BF 109 AND ITS CONTEMPORARIES

TYPE	Bf 109B-2	Bf 109E-3	Bf 109F-4	Bf 109G-6	Bf 109K-4	Fw 190 A-3	North American P-51 D
Year Built	III/37	IV/39	III/41	I/43	Iv/44	II/42	I/43
Power Plant	Jumo 210 Da	DB 601 Aa	Db 601 E-1	DB 605 AM	DB 605 D	BMW 801 D	Packard V-1650-7 Merlin
Takeoff Power	680 HP	1175 HP	1350 HP	1475 HP	2000 HP	1700 HPtb	1695 HP
Performance	640 HP at 2700 m	1100 HP at 4500 m	1300 HP at 5500 m	1700 HP at 4100 m (MW 50)	1355 HP at 5700 m, 1800 HP at 5000 m	1440 HP at 5800 m	not available
Speed	410 kph at sea level 470 kph at 4000 m	470 kph at sea level 560 kph at 4400 m	540 kph a sea level 570 kph at 6500 m	550 kph at sea level with M 50 620 kph at 6900 m	610 kph at sea level with M 50 725 kph at 7600 m	500 kph at sea level	600 kph at sea level 700 kph at 7600 m
Maximum Range	690 km	660 km	850 km with drop tank	560 km, 1000 km with drop tank		800 km	1500 km, 3300570 kmkm with drop tanks
Empty Weight	1500 kg	1900 kg	2400 kg	2700 kg	2700 kg	2900 kg	3200 Kg
Maximum Weight	2150 kg	2700 kg	3100 kg	3400 kg	3400 kg	4000 kg	5500 kg
Length	8.55 m	8.65 m	8.85 m	8.90 m	8.85 m	8.80 m	9.83 m
Wingspan	9.87 m	9.87 m	9.91 m	9.92 m	9.98 m	10.51 m	11.28 m
Armament	two MG 17 (7.92 mm) in fuselage, one MG 18 between cylinder banks	two MG 17 (7.92 mm) in fuselage, two MG FF (s in fuselage, 20 mm) in wing	two MG 17, (7.92 mm) in fuselage one MG 151 (20 mm) between cylinder banks, various equipment kits'	two MG 131 (13 mm) two MG 151 (20 mm) in fuselage, one MG 151 (20 mm), between cylinder banks in underwing gondolas, various equipment kits	two MG 131 (13 mm) in fuselage, one MK 108 (30 mm) in between cylinder banks various equipment kit	two MG 17 (7.9 mm) in fuselage two MG 151 - and two MG FFi in wings, various equipment kit	six MG 53 (12.7) machine guns in the wings, various external stores